PAUL FARLEY was born                   and studied at the Chelsea School of A           ished five collections of poetry with Picador, mos     ntly *The Mizzy* (2019), as well as *Selected Poems* (2014). His other books include *Edgelands* (co-authored with Michael Symmons Roberts, 2011) and an edited selection of John Clare's poetry. A Fellow of the Royal Society of Literature and a frequent broadcaster, he has received numerous awards including *Sunday Times* Young Writer of the Year, the Whitbread Poetry Prize and the E.M. Forster Award from the American Academy of Arts & Letters.

*Also by Paul Farley*

The Mizzy

Selected Poems

The Dark Film

Tramp in Flames

The Ice Age

The Boy from the Chemist is Here to See You

*Paul Farley*

# When It Rained for a Million Years

PICADOR

First published 2025 by Picador
an imprint of Pan Macmillan
The Smithson, 6 Briset Street, London EC1M 5NR
*EU representative:* Macmillan Publishers Ireland Ltd, 1st Floor,
The Liffey Trust Centre, 117–126 Sheriff Street Upper,
Dublin 1, D01 YC43
Associated companies throughout the world
www.panmacmillan.com

ISBN 978-1-0350-6867-8

Copyright © Paul Farley 2025

The right of Paul Farley to be identified as the
author of this work has been asserted by him in accordance
with the Copyright, Designs and Patents Act 1988.

All rights reserved. No part of this publication may be reproduced,
stored in a retrieval system, or transmitted, in any form, or by any means
(electronic, mechanical, photocopying, recording or otherwise)
without the prior written permission of the publisher.

The Notes and Acknowledgments on page 81 constitute
an extension of this copyright page.

Pan Macmillan does not have any control over, or any responsibility for,
any author or third-party websites referred to in or on this book.

1 3 5 7 9 8 6 4 2

A CIP catalogue record for this book is available from the British Library.

Printed and bound by CPI (UK) Ltd, Croydon CR0 4YY

This book is sold subject to the condition that it shall not, by way of
trade or otherwise, be lent, hired out, or otherwise circulated without
the publisher's prior consent in any form of binding or cover other than
that in which it is published and without a similar condition including
this condition being imposed on the subsequent purchaser.

Visit www.picador.com to read more about all our books
and to buy them. You will also find features, author interviews and
news of any author events, and you can sign up for e-newsletters
so that you're always first to hear about our new releases.

*In memory of Freda Romaya*

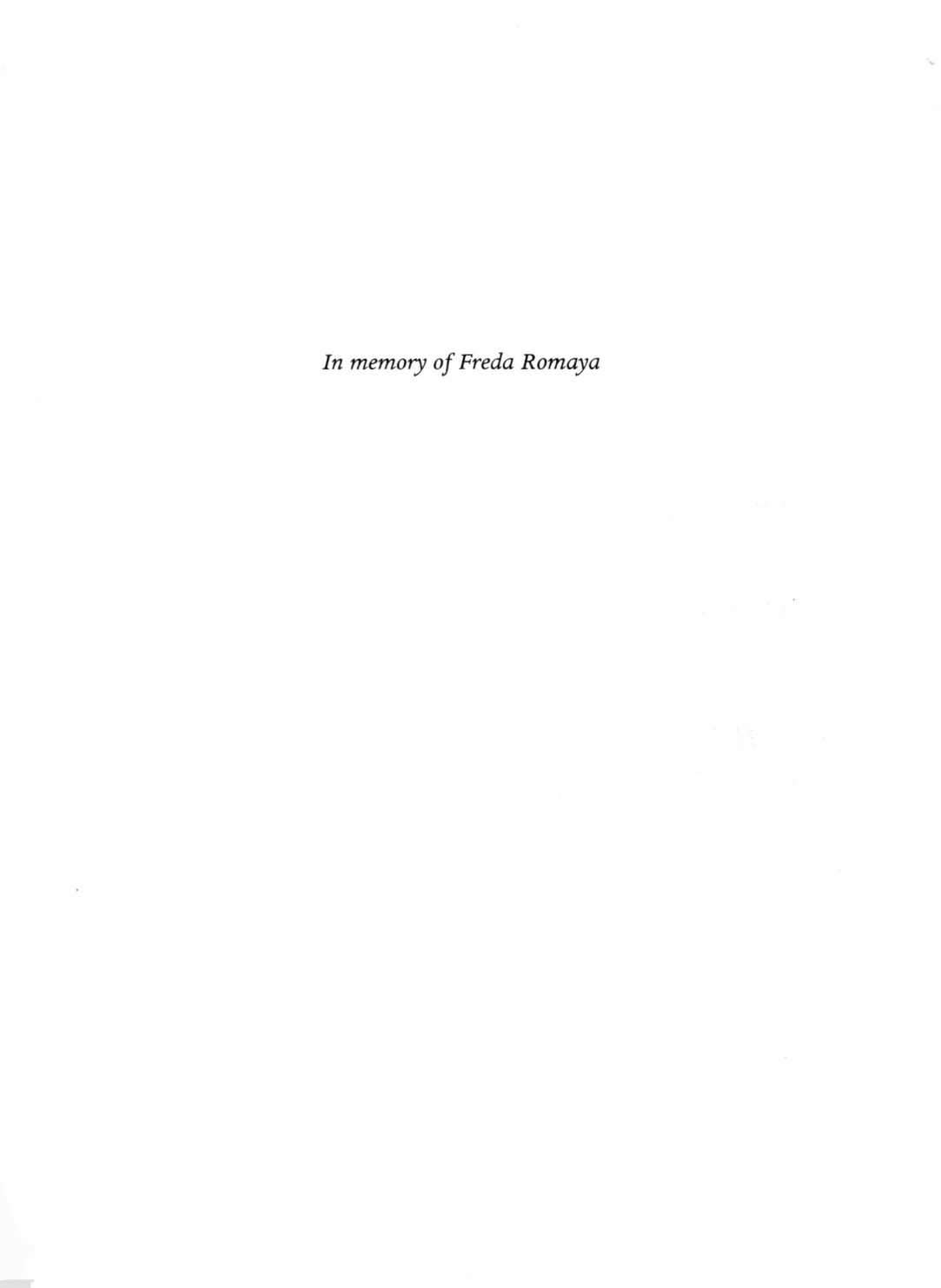

# Contents

## 1

Planesong  3

Ink  6

Source  7

King Carbon  8

Attack of the Fifty-Foot Poem  10

First Foot  11

The Enemy  12

Our Father Who Showed Us Sea Level  13

Three Rings  14

Close Reading  16

Three Riots  18

Tumbleweed  20

The Rout at Brunanburh  21

The Block  22

A Room  24

Guide  26

In One of Your Urgent Poems  27

The Superflag  28

## 2

The Gorilla  33

A Rewilding  34

Horde  35

Turkeys  36

Conger Eel  37

Wagtail Roost, Cheshire Oaks Outlet Village  38

The Workaround  39

Corncrakes  41

Swifts  42

The Horse  44

Great Northern Diver  46

Dragonfly  47

## 3

Usher  51

Difficult to Enter House  56

Slush  57

The Execution of Anne Boleyn, Airfix 1:12  59

Myths  60

Where the Owl Sleeps and the Spiders Nest  62

Trth   63

Tinned Peaches   64

The Studio   68

Mascara   69

Memories of Midhope Street   70

Night Class   72

My Last Drink   73

Cross Bedding, Between Edge Hill and Lime Street   74

∞   76

Bubblewrap   77

*Notes*   81

*Acknowledgements*   83

# When It Rained for a Million Years

1

# Plancsong

Listen to that. My favourite sound.
It finds more space to fill
at night, to resonate in,
to overwrite the day
just gone, that tuning down,
that fall in pitch that doesn't really fall
at all. Like a wave thing,
an unravelling.
   Every day should end
with a light aircraft passing overhead,
not the airliner's crumbling
distant landslip, more
a sound that heals itself,
or seals itself.
   I heard it from my bed
in the house by the Edge Hill sidings,
airy above the shunt and clank
of earthbound trains.
I was full of age and longing
even though I was young
and knew next to nothing.
Full of elsewhere. I learned to make it last
like peeling an apple until
the peel touches the ground.
I listen now and it winds me back
to that earliest core –
a transistor crackle in air

that smelled of iron and coal,
passengers yards away
travelling through their 1968
on the blackened side of a railway wall.
We each have our bearings.
   Is this a classical plane
crop-dusting the fields or streets we start out from?
The same 'eternal note of sadness'
or 'lacrimae rerum note' –
though getting quotey breaks the spell,
like the plane trails a message.
Can we not just listen for a minute?
   Sometimes I personify it:
the way a scribbled palm summons a bill
or a hand wafted across the throat
will cut the engine of speech,
I picture a sky god, like Tin,
stretching tight an invisible cord
making the sign to draw things out, to *fill* . . .
and everything I've been taught
about travelling the furthest distance
in the fewest words, economy, concision,
goes out the window
along with these items: a flint lighter's smell
of metal and petrol,
the word 'Zippo',
frictionless borders,
film stock fogged in an age of bomb tests,
old maps in drawers,
cassette tape worn to a hiss,

kitchen windows steamed by a ham broth,
pen pals behind the Iron Curtain . . .
    But listen to me drone on. I wonder now
if anyone else hears this plane,
a Cessna travelling inbound for Speke,
a Piper in the clouds on a wet night
drawing its bow of rain,
and if they do, what that might mean,
and who is being dreamed up.
Sound bending back
towards its source, the sound that was just here
by now already out over the sea,
*now* falling into *then* and back again
to reach you,
even though you're fast asleep.

# Ink

A word begins in the wind
a scribe thinks, and, thinking,
his hand slips. His mind
enters a gap between scratching
and nib taps. The lamp flickers. Owls
screech in the top woods.
He holds his breath. His soul
is looking down at the words
and the word he tripped on
looks back, puzzled, like it dwells
on distances – between dip
and driving quill, the ground
it's put between ports and turf smoke,
the flights over frozen lands,
flinty waves, the dark narrows it took
to reach here. The scribe's hand
hovers above the page
where he left it, waiting to be found
and grasped again – the village
rising slowly, the cold side of a bed
he'll retire to after the first bell
or cockcrow, the small hours'
rows and columns stacked –
but before the ink goes everywhere
the word looks back, holding him still,
and he listens down, for as long
as he dares, into a deep well
that's swallowed his tongue.

# Source

Characters *are* the story, somebody wrote,
and a character we can root for gives us plot.
A girl and boy with slate-grey eyes and cracked lips
lie on their bellies drinking from a puddle.
We're in the close third-person so we know
how they filter this water, drawing it up
through the voices of their grandparents – backstory
emerges out of character – who ran
the tap each morning and listened to it drum
into a kettle, summoned from the main
with little thought for reservoirs in the hills
or navvies upstream in the past, or women
in that same moment balancing oil cans
the mile home from a muddy ditch. This girl
and boy are so thirsty we root for them,
their quest for clear water, their prayers for rain,
and like the greatest characters in fiction
they emerge out of the wellspring of real people,
even though a character's source isn't important
to the reader – only what is there on the page.

# King Carbon

A King who wakes on a bed of coal
and rises to many demands:

snow to the north, heatwaves to the south,
boom and growth all around.

A King who ordered his palace torched
so he'd feel more at home,

who looks at the overnight reports
on a charred and scaly throne.

Who sets prices and weighs the threats
from wind and sun and tide.

Who wields a diamond-hard pencil
when given decrees to sign.

Who's a merry old soul, always cracking up,
murdering his own crude jokes

as he rolls in soot with his concubines
then CH=CH=CH=chain-smokes.

Who dines on kippers and carbonara,
drinks wines with a nose of gunflint

with his Queen from the House of Hydrogen,
each in the other's element . . .

Is it fun to build a King like this,
like a snowman or a scarecrow

you could banish to the undergloom
where giant fronds of fern grow?

Does it help to build a King like this,
a jokey, smoky sovereign

removed from power to a cooling tower
on the eve of demolition?

A guy you could throw on a bonfire
and dance around in a ring.

Or would you make a loyal subject
and live in a world of things?

Or would you shiver, poor and cold
in the court of a carbon king?

## Attack of the Fifty-Foot Poem

Dismantled in the long workshop of history,
the poem lies in state. By candlelight
aldermen and professors and the like
pay their respects. When they let the public in
there is a tiny queue. Not like a fire sale
and people kipping on pavements. Just a trickle
that files into St George's civic gloom
slowly, stewarded, at first light.
And here, as we approach the fiftieth foot
that no one needs to know falls at *this point*,

the poem breaks step. It comes to life.
It rises! *Where are my readers?*
*Is this it? You?* It speaks! Active poem panic.
It crawls from the hall, minding its head
as it pokes through the Corinthian columns
like a dog from a neoclassical kennel,
blinking and sniffing the air. It drags out its hindquarters.
The sandstone lions grind their teeth and look on.
Crowds are pointing and screaming *Poem!*
It makes the ground shake. It recites!
It climbs St John's Beacon, pleasuring itself
and flinging its own muck at the grant funding bodies.

# First Foot

It's the first few seconds of the year.
Those screams are distant fireworks.
That's the lowing of ships' horns on the river.
This is a man pulling on his boots.
This man is going moonlighting,
working nights just for one night,
carrying no ladders or tools or columned book.
This man isn't coming to collect,
take names, tell anyone they're in arrears.
This is a midnight where debts and bad blood
are at their furthest point from the sun.
This man is certain to be met
with a smoke or a drink at every door,
welcomed into his neighbours' arms,
into their alien atmospheres:
off-gassing carpets, the ghost of a roast,
wet dog fur . . . He can't know yet
that this is the final year he'll see in
but let's not get ahead of ourselves
or him. Look how he laces his boots
slowly, in his own time, making it last.

# The Enemy

*after Baudelaire*

My youth was belts of cloud and thunderstorms
broken by sweet spots or suntraps
but the rumblings and the rain were so full on
the currants in our yard rarely grew ripe.
It's autumn now. I'm out of ideas
and I've a need for a rake and a spade,
to put my back into the waterlogged earth.
Sometimes it feels like digging my own grave.
And will I find the bulbs of those flowers
that glowed on grey days like a submerged reef,
running on their own mysterious power,
or will he cut right through the mains supply,
my own worst enemy, that other I
who draws down from the circuit of my life.

# Our Father Who Showed Us Sea Level

The world had weighed anchor. The docks were deserted.
We took turns on his shoulders to look at sea level
there, carved in the sea wall, slick and green.
*The heights and depths of the world are measured from here . . .*
It went over our heads. I remember marks
in the stone, a salty, solder smell, being sick
on the bus going home. The heights and depths of the world?
Its mountains and mineshafts, skyscrapers, canyons?

Turned out he was half right, maybe not even half
as I learned myself further away from him,
as the idea of the absolute datum point,
the line in the sand, the seeing things in black and white,
recedes. The glaciers melt, the moon hauls gravel,
even the land itself rises and falls.

I'm drawing a line under it all – our father,
who didn't rule the waves or make the rules,
who must have been a believer in sea level
on some level, who lifted me from the bus,
not eight feet high but wrapped, like the child I was,
in a donkey jacket rough with smoke and rain –

drawing a line and leaving it like a pilgrim
who's waited long enough, home from the cave
or sea grotto where once, in an apparition,
some saw the heights of devotion, the depths of love.

# Three Rings

Struggling to remember who wrote
'The Telephone Number of the Muse',
I get put through instead to the ritual
of three rings, that signal

our loved ones had made it home
and the long day could come
to a close. Ellipses, cues
for the lights to be put out

across the city – for all I knew
towards all points north-westerly –
in the settled silence that followed.
I'd forgotten this folky telecoms curfew.

I'd forgotten being so thrifty.
I'd forgotten the pre-text etiquette
everyone understood, this code
that removed whole areas of doubt

from the night. I let it ring three times
when drink-dialling our old house
to let my parents know I've arrived
and they can stop worrying now:

the ivory handset under the stairs,
the stopped chime hanging in the air
as the knickknacks and souvenirs look on . . .
All of it ex-directory, gone.

Even the blank exchange, busy as a mill
switching and pulsing behind
its rain-stained concrete bulwarks,
the thing that connected us all,

and I seem to have brought us to a dark
industrial building where love's never been
which isn't where I wanted this to land
and not what I want it to mean.

# Close Reading

Your favourite stretch in Dickens
wasn't the meeting on the marshes
or the ghost out of the future,

but Oliver's flight from Mudfog
and the road south to London,
maybe because you were restless –

not put upon or starved
like poor Oliver, but walking away
from that life was a plausible adventure:

a crust of bread, a coarse shirt, the high road
of the M62 they were just building
the doorway to another world,

whatever. This passage lay hidden
but load-bearing for many years
until you heard of the Mudfog affair,

a scholarly rumble on its whereabouts
which shifted your foundations
when travelling the Great North Road,

passing through Peterborough Services,
eating at The Gandhi in Sandy,
brooding on fenland outside Stilton,

all on the trail of the poet John Clare
who had walked north from the asylum
eating grass, steering by the Pole star,

who might have met a pale thin boy
coming the other way, nursing blisters,
lice in his hems, crust in the seat

of his britches, which nobody mentions;
they might have shared a pipe by a milestone,
asking each other what led them here

and look what's happened . . . A meeting,
a landscape, a ghost from the future.
You're hungry now and want to go home.

# Three Riots

2011 and 1990 and 1981
are tucked up safely in their beds.
There are no difficult dreams of smoke
or black batons or screams
creasing a brow or raising a pillow sweat.

I'm tiptoeing around
and don't want them waking up.
That would lead to an inquiry.
Besides, it took ages to get them down
with their favourite stories.

1981 likes to hear
the tale about me being sixteen
and happening upon plastic shields
stacked against the railings
in Hope Street, some speckled with blood.

With 1990, I barely get beyond
the beginning: how I followed a noise
into Trafalgar Square – thrown traffic cones,
the clatter of the horses
charging – before its eyes close.

2011 grows heavy lidded as I describe
a metal smell, a hotel window
open on a summer night
as a warehouse burned, and there are no
protests when I smile and put out the light.

# Tumbleweed

*O will I have nothing to show for the long miles*
a tumbleweed wonders, a dandelion clock
that emigrated, did well, grew huge, blew back
a legend of the screen, though there were tales
about a lack of lines leading to trouble
and rumours of unhappy sets, a broom
without a handle bumbling through each frame.
Affairs with creosote-scented chaparral
were toxic box office, too. But all that gossip,
Vegas, wilderness years, even the straitened
landscapes of TV, mean plenty of work
in the empty air that follows certain jokes,
or miles of nothing when a line doesn't land,
and someone wishes the ground would open up.

# The Rout at Brunanburh

Knackered Northmen, lucky lads
who scattered before they got skewered,
clamber into nail-studded boats
in the creek by the Thing
and do one, for deep draughts and Ireland
across the sea . . .
                If some tend
the wounded with poultices and splints,
or try and fail to kindle a song,
or blink back the look of bafflement
on a face they split from brow to throat,
or weep for a horse, now there's time for that
under shameful sail – we'll never know.

The chronicle steers back towards
the meat of the matter. The kites. The crows.

# The Block

After one last scrub
they could burn you like Rosebud
or flog you on eBay,
too gravid and weighty

to end up as kindling,
though chopping seems fitting –
the blows of the big blades,
the hackwork of decades.

A tablet recording
the boning, the scoring,
the workmanlike dicing,
the paring, the slicing . . .

You don't have to answer
but next to the mincer
and scales all these years
is it true what I've heard

that you've seen off four butchers
who each left their signatures,
stilettoes on dancefloors
notating a night before

like patterns in nature,
though of all the creatures
or pieces of creatures
called in from the pastures

next-to-nothing remains
bar these deep copper stains.
Is it true you're self-healing?
That you haven't got feelings?

If blood could run backwards
we could find the exact woods
upstream, where the lambs
run in frail little gangs

and calves in their dreamtime
are grazing in half-rhymes,
where the woodcutter earmarks
a tree in its soft bark

returning in autumn
to reap you. Imagine
beginning with an axe blow.
Blows being all you'll ever know.

# A Room

Today, you could run the whole thing from a laptop
in any coffee chain with decent Wi-Fi,
but back then I ran poetry from a room
above a bookmaker's. I had three phones
plumbed in and used a PO Box down the road,
registered as a charity, took out a loan.
Ushered inside, visitors couldn't believe
my operations room, this nerve centre
with its auction-bought swivel chairs, its files
in soul-destroying livers and cyans,
the well-appointed rooms they had in mind
dismantled right behind their very eyes
to accommodate the thrashed yucca, that tin
of fly spray rusting on the dusty sill.

It used to be a cab office, and I left
the map up on the wall. Its YOU ARE HERE
had been 'heavily shelled by drawing pins'
one visiting poet said, smiling to himself.
What did people expect? What kind of room
should lie at the difficult heart of things?
The shadow of the building opposite
did lend it a bunker's noonday gloom,
but they struggled with the groaning copier
and racing from Uttoxeter downstairs.
At dusk, the cabstand's beacon still came on
'like a sped-up lighthouse' the poet said.
I couldn't wait to show him to the door.
*Goodbye*. I had a business to run.

# Guide

My interior has a guide. Look,
they say. A city street
in summer, one of those days
when the crowds have thinned out
and everyone has gone to the beach;
a young mother left behind, her kids
running in circles around a bench
where she sparks up a ciggie; the buses
locked in their timetables; the smell
of hot pavements and cooking oil,
a sunstruck emptiness
broken suddenly by a man
who is shouting at nothing, walking
and roaring, air-drumming his fists
and throwing his head back. The kids
squinch in to their mother, frightened,
and the guide doesn't know how to put this
but, well, that man is me. I don't think so.
The guide can see my shock. We
look nothing like each other. Look
again, the guide says. And, fuck me

# In One of Your Urgent Poems

It was like being the *I* in one of your urgent poems,
an *I* that moved dreamlike with strange purpose.
A drunk *I*, still stupefied from a club,
swaying home on autopilot. A fox
*I* trapped by its instincts in a security light.

An italic *I* tilted like a lance,
or like a pole-vaulter on the run up,
which is more of a backslash \ and for which
there is no glyph, not even in the poem's Unicode.
It was good being *I*, making zero sense.

Virgule, diagonal, solidus . . .
*I* was in that line up. You know what ruined it?
Police radios. He wanted to stay longer
but it turns out *I* is a terrible anchor
(not like the grapnel of J or the hitch knot of Q).

He was *him* again, on the ground,
wet through his jeans, gravel in his mouth,
voices telling him *calm down*,
blue-gloved hands going through his pockets
searching for any form of ID.

# The Superflag

We watch it fill the giant screen
        and hear it behind us, tacking like sail,
                a rumour with a definite edge.

We're watching and can *feel* its approach,
        floating with the acreage
                of empty commercial premises.

We think of how it shivers like
        a bolt of silk on a bed of nails,
                or a waterfall in a pantomime.

Then it pauses. It has a mind of its own
        or has the mind of a swarm or shoal.
                We feel its overcast and the hairs

on the backs of our necks are magnetized.
        Our arms rise and we all become
                part of one giant bedsheet ghost.

We scare ourselves when we look around.
        We see the big screen through its shroud.
                We see the floodlamps as four moons.

We see its leaf veins, running repairs.
        In this world with different gravity
                there's a definite pull. Look at our hands

waving like starfish on a tide.
    There's held breath, like when the shot glass
        on a talking board begins to slide

and when we emerge on the other side
    and out from under it, we cheer,
        while the fans in the away end sing:

Where's your famous
    Where's your famous
        *Where's your famous atmosphere?*

2

# The Gorilla

*The meeting host will let you in soon . . .*
Here in the lobby, in limbo, waiting to gain
entry, before another Zoom call
gets underway, I rehearse, a screen actor,
only this time, there, in the speaker thumbnail,
rendered an eye-blink slower than my own,
is another face. Time is out of joint.
Latency. The lag in the machine. I
look behind the 'now' our brain predicts
a split second before the next thing happens,
which this face must be gurning in the middle of
all the time, never meeting my eye, a shy
latent mug a moment ago, and I
keep blinking my dad, about my age, alive
in this moment. The other guy – the one with
no creases or crow's feet, no silvery
grey hair, the gob that greets me in the slowest mirrors,
the me I kid myself I am – he's gone.
'Hello?' The host has let me into the meeting
room, and look how quickly we slip into
our roles, how much slips through the gaps, how
unknowable things are, how quickly our time
goes, how misdirection masks the truth,
how we never see the gorilla walking through.

# A Rewilding

Masonic creature. Maker. Water encircled
survivor of hat crazes. Crib fabricator.
Chiseller. Tooth enamel's hardest expression
on any branch of the mammal clade. Stash house
builder. Stickler. Worker in wands and twigs,
in waterproof slick fur. Dammer of the catchment
under winter constellations that burn and flicker
when dark and frost resume the Northern hemisphere.
Your ice creche. Your infinity pool of the woods.
Your gnawing that forks panic through the sap.
Your assault on the vertical. Busybody at rest
locked in your latticework, the birch tar scent
of Shalimar locked in you – how could any forest
forget such a creature? You need no introduction.

# Horde

We were in a kind of big industrial shed.
They were using lights to keep us in rhythm.
We were fed with bales of dry stuff. There'd be fights
to get the choice soft centre. We drank from a gutter
and fought for the highest place – those at the end
of the incline caught the most slobber and spit.
There was a lot of rucking in the stalls
and it didn't help that they played Joy Division
or The Human League at full blast, that the lights
would strobe sometimes. They gave us antibiotics.
The steel barriers would rattle. They played Bowie –
the Berlin trilogy – and sluiced the concrete floor.
We stomped. The roof groaned under the weight of snow
then sang as it thawed. We lowed. There was no answer.
Then one day without warning the sky came in
through hangar doors. Our gas escaped. We followed
each other towards the light, spattered and trembling,
into the field, which was there, as long rumoured,
jumping and kicking in ways we weren't designed to,
some breaking into gallops and many kneeling
to rub their faces in the sweet wet grasses.

# Turkeys

One with a shock of bollock wattle
and the quick eyes of a Shadow Minister for Agriculture and
 Livestock
pokes its neck in. 'Before we move forward
I for one would like to understand what we're dealing with here.'

One with lobes as red as a Rouge Coco lipstick
raises its head. 'It's called Christmas. It's a human event.'

The Shadow Minister flaps its snood and gobbles. 'We know,
but *what* do we know? We feel the sheds
growing overcrowded and loud, the pecking worse
as the days shorten, but what's the deal with Christmas?'

One enormous Bronze tom weighs in. 'They are celebrating the birth
of their saviour, who was born in a shed too.' The Shadow Minister
blushes, engorged. 'So, all this for a poult?'

'The poult *Jesus*,' answers the Bronze tom, eyeballing nothing
in the shavings then scratching it furiously. Rouge Coco burbles to
 think
of the little poult on starter pellets. The Shadow Minister
turns to the flock. 'And was the poult Jesus slaughtered at twenty-
 four weeks?'

Uproar. Flapping of lobes. *No!* The Shadow Minister
has them. Sideways strut. Flirted fan. 'Let's put it to a vote.'

## Conger Eel

Angelfish and piranhas
dazzle us. You live in a wreck
down the end of the corridor,

so it's said. A few get lured
by a mystery in native waters – believers
in local depths – who put their heads

in your cloud of green murk. Kids,
who think 'the conga' is a dance
inspired by you – it kind of makes sense –

or build eels from tinned sardines,
an inch of oil to the mile of saltwater
at teatime. Some show patience

before a tiny haunted Atlantic,
are given a bead of bubbles to revere
from a porthole that leads nowhere

but you never put in an appearance.
You're the god of no-shows.
Staring into your tank like a shop window

is me doing it wrong. And when
the lights flicker off and on it only means
the aquarium will be closing soon.

## Wagtail Roost, Cheshire Oaks Outlet Village

During the three-day reign
of a March storm, under the rule
of a tyrant, a cold blowhard,

they gather and huddle
in trees planted to soften
and rusticate the retail park

and survive the night, a few feet
from a designer store,
keeping warm on what we leak,

a draft under the doors
of longhouse and feasting hall,
our handbags against the dark.

# The Workaround

We took it to Bede
and he came up with a workaround.
At first he struggled to get his head around
glass that big. True, there were furnaces
at Jarrow, but his was a world
of nooks and vents, shutters and flaps.
Our world of windows and shiny surfaces
took some explaining. We stood a still lake on its side
till he got the picture and got his head in the game,

marvelling at what English had been up to:
that little bird he knew by a Dark Age name
here a *spadger*, there a *spuggie*, plastic and molten
then cooling and hardening into Latin,
then living with the martin, the mouse
and the fly, under the common roof of 'house'.
He was brought up to speed
with bird strike and windowkill, sad
to see his bird double-glazed out of its parable.

We told him the workforce couldn't bear to look
at another pigeon's archeopteryx
ghosted on the glass. He agreed that thud
of feathers was bad for morale.
He thought long and hard on a fix,
scratching his itchy clerical beard,
his mind fluttering like a bird at a pane,
his brain hot in a smokehouse of thought,
and finally said: Ingress! Egress!

Translated, he meant: Throw open the windows!
Old world warblers, swifts and swallows,
muscle-keeled geese with their line managers
could pass over hot desk and shared printer,
through conditioned air, only sensing us
as a glitch in the planet's guidance.
But we can't take a proposal based
on visions and dreams to the people upstairs.
And he said, you have to, while there's still a chance.

# Corncrakes

When you hear them, why does it feel like coming home?
Where you grew up, they'd long gone. Then it clicks
and you remember: those television shows
where any EXT: NIGHT was dubbed with crickets
and cicadas, but throw open the window
to listen, and nothing: a shout, a van up the road.

*It's not for the common birds that I'd mourn* . . . It's hard
to tell the calls apart or judge their distance.
Midnight's *creak creak*. A sound recordist once
warned you corncrakes would do your head in
and they do, but not in the way you think she meant.
The late light in the west makes the sound more ancient

and your mum and dad are alive. You're watching *Columbo*
or *The Streets of San Francisco*. These are young males
from last summer, returned to the nettle bed
or set-aside they were born in, and might be dead
this time next year, so sing for hours on end.
The song is bigger than them. That's all they know.

# Swifts

Some get Brunelleschi's dome
in Florence. The campaniles of Rome
might greet them when they arrive home
after the long flight north.

Others get the chimneystacks
of a Ruhr town, or radio masts,
or the swing bridge at Preston Docks.
Swifts weren't put on this earth

to care much either way; they scream,
last to arrive and first to leave –
our hollow walls and broken eaves
the only earth they know.

I'm hearing what I want to hear.
To live life on the wing, not care
for worldly things, at home in air.
I've wished that I could follow

the swifts south, but the other way
the wish is truer, harder. They
take to the skies as stowaways
to fly north into green.

On the descent into Heathrow
a frostbitten man (who's never seen snow)
in an Airbus wheel well finally lets go
and falls towards East Sheen.

# The Horse

We lived with a horse
and he kept us in oats.
Each morning we woke
to his kicks and his snorts,
the length of his horse piss,
the brass of his farts,
then rose once he'd left
for the field where he worked

where we thought he was running
for guineas, for gold,
where we thought he was jumping
the fence of the world,
not ploughing a scrubby old
plot in the cold,
or hitched to a cart
or being used on the road.

We'd hear him come home
kicking off his horseshoes
and could smell his horse sweat
as he cleared his horse lungs
with a cough at the sink
and sometimes he'd sing
or might roll in the straw
or might swish away stings

and we shovelled his horseshit
and did our own thing
although sometimes the scars
of the saddle and whip
made him mean so we learned
when to give him the slip,
when to test his horsepower,
or give him some lip

until visits from vets
and then *we* kept a horse
in an unstable stable
and when he got worse
he would fall like a foal,
so we moved him downstairs
and we fed him and sponged him
and took it in turns

and I can't speak for them
but there's times when I wished
we could shoot him, and wept,
and by now you'll have guessed
that there was no horse
and there was no straw,
but this wish marked the start
of the whole metaphor.

# Great Northern Diver

Listen. Big divers calling at twilight,
home for their annual refit on a sea loch,
bobbing like grids of floats that cage
salmon in their farms, or mark a wreck,
breaking the silent routine of night
coming on. Say what you like,
there are no words. Say it's where birdsong
begins. Say you're standing at the edge
of this water when the world was young.
Say it breaks the surface of our age.
Say it stands us in the middle of things.
Say it overdubs the sound of what's
to come – not tonight, but soon – and sends
a ripple through your heart. *It's not
all about you* . . . Say it's where birdsong ends.

# Dragonfly

You're going to die soon,
race run, job done,
white soft oiled eggs deposited

in the green matrix of a pool.

Now it's all about waiting for frost.
You hover, dart, go through
the pitch and yaw of kills

and all for what? Today, in a watery noon,
you caught yourself staring into time,

sunning on a stone. Fossilized.
You and your shadow actual size.

You've had these wings since giants
walked the earth, or grew,
so, you're going to see what they can do.

Your wreckage, your debris strewn,
your fuselage and mantle
lost in the oxblood-spotted docks,
or ditched in a cold pond –

none of this matters to you.
You've set a course for the sun.

If you leave now, you'll have a clear run.
Let's see what these babies can do.

3

# Usher

*Tampoco puedo explicarme por qué sueño*
*con pilas de linternas*
— Ricardo Zelarayán

*The Color of Money*

A sad faced boy from Brazil
even lonelier than I am in London
splits shifts with me and shares
the cupboard off the foyer that smells
of mop buckets and cologne
where we change between shows.
He teaches me some Portuguese in passing.
*Baterias? Da sua lanterna?*

*Look Who's Talking*

I check the batteries on my torch.
I'm going in. Through heavy doors
into the big dark where soundtracks roost.
I guide punters, down aisles and rows,
lighting the way, finding their seats.
I'm wearing a necklace of ticket stubs.
The trailers boom like a tropical storm.

*Ghost*

There are always latecomers,
and my job is to lead them in
then out as stragglers when the credits crawl,
but sometimes I think my real role
is to move between different realities
and know where all the exits are.
Playing cards with the projectionist
in his booth is like being a ghost
sitting outside of running time.
The manager sending me out to the kiosk
for his Standard – it has to be
the West End Final – is always a shock,
the light of the world, the evening traffic
having no idea what's going on inside.

*Do the Right Thing*

I check the batteries on my torch.
I'm going in again. Who or what
led me here to play this old part,
the meeter and greeter at the door,
the one who leads the way and walks before,
the one who invites the faithful forward,
the one who smiles at the threshold.
The adverts roar like a desert storm.

*Die Hard*

This is my first fatherless job.
Fitting that it comes with a big torch:
I'd lost my way along a hospital's
bright corridors, strayed from my lane.
Outside, the traffic had no idea
what was going on inside.
I walked for miles. I took a train.
The weather broke. The seasons changed.
I saw an ad. I picked up the baton.
Sometimes in the movies' deepest lulls
I'll grip my hand over its bulb.
My fingers glow like in the womb.

*Field of Dreams*

I wish I knew what I was watching.
A scruffy drifter arrives in town.
Someone gets stuck inside a cave.
Someone finds then loses love.
A dreamer trapped in a dead end job
ushers in a new era of something.
A family gathers at a bedside.
There is a close-up of a held hand.

*The Untouchables*

Work really begins after THE END.
The last drunk is shaken and shown the door.
I root under the seats with my dust pan
and plastic bin bag, looking for a story
in the crowded emptiness of an auditorium
with the house lights up, in my uniform
that smells of mops and turns me invisible.
Kleenex. Popcorn. Orange peel.

*Moonstruck*

Back at the surface after my shift,
at the coal face of the box office,
years will pass. I'm going to forget this.
One day the light will pass straight through it,
the films that rumbled gone, like thunder
in childhood. I won't even wonder
what became of the boy from Brazil.

*Rain Man*

The last thing I do is switch off the lights
and pull down the shutters. I set the alarm,
leaving a gap in the metal blinds
to duck under. And in the time
it takes to get clear, as time counts down,
I look back at the space I've made
in the city. I do this every night.
Outside, the air is thick with fumes
and rain and anything is about
to happen.

# Difficult to Enter House

Grafting together, we spent most of that first
winter unbolting squats, foraging in skips,
entering the bank to ask for an overdraft
and drawing on its smell – beeswax and money –
and I remember when they said they'd stop
our cards, freeze our accounts, you'd use your gift
to fold a paying-in slip into a flower
and offer it to them. Now the bank's a phone shop
and we lost touch years ago. But today I passed
a doorway which I never knew was there
and thought of you again. This is why I stop
to feel the blood-warm brickwork, why I slip
my arm around the trunk of this young tree.

# Slush

Maybe you're owed an ode. Maybe you're feeling
hard done by. Maybe snow and rain have bossed it
and had things to themselves for so long, your cold
sulk can be explained.

So, you're getting this. *Hush now little slushman . . .*
but as I give you human form you're going
the way of all slush: you won't take shape and hold,
and here come the greys

of blown bulbs, seascapes, the darkest daytime skies
known to winter ponds, all concrete, certain clays;
the grime of the age that hides in wheel arches
revealed, our exhaust

brought down to earth and ramified by tyres,
manifest in footfall, churned to a shallow
quagmire. You're a landscape that needs to go
straight into the wash

though can be pure and driven: packed in chest holes
around stopped hearts; and can deliver brain freeze
in the foyer of a different theatre.
You've always been here:

the bow wave of the glacier's creep that ploughs
earth and grit; hooves jostling in a midden.
Hard goings and long droves. The ruts of armies
advancing. Mostly

you're elegiac because of your retreat
under a clearing sky, the way you move on
and, after a last few dirty looks, have gone,
quickly forgotten

on the streets you occupied. We get a grip,
surefooted in an order out of chaos.
Don't sulk. You didn't give me much to work with
but you're getting this.

# The Execution of Anne Boleyn, Airfix 1:12

                face and hood
                            back of hood
              front of gown
                            back of gown
    supporting plaque and veil
                            display plinth and earth
        front right arm and cuff
                            rear right arm
                right hand
                            front of pedestal
              rear of pedestal
                            sundial
                  gnomon
                            front left arm and cuff
              rear left arm
                            left hand
                rose flower
                            rose stem
              frond of ivy
                            frond of ivy
                  ivy leaf
                          ivy leaf
            handkerchief

# Myths

First off, let's have it right: it wasn't the sun
but cold. A contrail is a comb of ice
a bear with hungry cubs in tow could cross
before it thaws. The beeswax didn't melt,
it turned glassy, till all my feathers seized
and stiffened but they withstood the stress test
of flight. Daedalus – I called him Dad for short –
did say: Don't go too high. Don't stay out late.
Don't test me. I was given a boy's wings
and gave the world a cautionary tale
however it's told – and Ovid tells it best,
though even he can't catch the utter boredom
of gathering wax from hives, feathers from nests,
three channels on TV, life happening
someplace else. The rest is total horseshit.
There were no flapping arms, no frantic tailspins
towards a shiny, concrete sea, no legs
pedalling air like Wile E. Coyote,
no diving headfirst into an old master
to make a hole in green water. I trimmed for glide
and brought myself down quietly.
                              And then
what happened is, the means of my escape,
the unimagined arts and natural laws
I brought to bear and broke to get me out
now break in me. You can hear me coming. Listen:
I rattle like a gourd, a bust kaleidoscope,

hailstone bingo inside a thundercloud,
and carry the handshake of a bottle bank.
*Put it there.* Cold as an ice bucket.
And Daedalus: they buried him with his tools
and ladders long ago. He drank his homebrew
and tinkered in the yard with scrap and grew
his dahlias, I'm told. Well-meaning tales
about him sat up late watching the night
to catch a port light blinking on a wing,
wondering if I was out there, safe from harm.
I used to think, when I saw the same thing:
*Some lucky bastard, going someplace warm.*

## Where the Owl Sleeps and the Spiders Nest

I'm idly wishing the end was more
like scoring a goal. That the final stroke
of the key or pen would lead to a knee slide
through mud, me running to the corner flag (which isn't there)
and punching it. That I'd do a little dance,
pull off my shirt and show my abs (which aren't there),
or do that thing that Cantona did and look
around me, regally, or salute the fans
in the stands, my crowds of readers (who aren't there).
I'm wishing it was more like that, instead
of this standing up and pacing a small room,
this abandonment, like the French poet said,
this open goal, this empty net, this game
where you never really know. I mean, do you?

# Trth

I lost my wedding ring on a reed bed
and went back to look. I made a wish
and retraced my steps, like the ring
might catch my eye, a needle

in a haystack kind of miracle.
Like I hadn't thought this thing through.
Like I'd lost the vowel from a solemn pledge
I had to renew. Like I expected

to find it threaded on a sedge
or along the tip of a bittern's bill,
worn as a cummerbund by an eel
or stuck like a lure in the mouth of a fish.

No, and no, and no, and no.
But I live in hope, say foolish things
and make it worse but don't mean to,
I do, I do, I do, I do.

# Tinned Peaches

*after Elinor Wylie*

1.

When the world completely goes to shit
you'll say the codeword – 'Innisfree!' –
and have a certain place in mind
two hours north, have requisitioned
washbasins from rocky dips
brim-full of rain, a row of trees
where clothes can dry in the westerlies
that crick them low. I can just see it:
the beck wired for trout, the fruit
that's sharp but sweetening under frost,
puddles that click, dandelion roots
brewed up as decaf, elderflowers steeped
into a tea to pick us up and keep
a cough from settling on our chests.

2.

A grab bag stuffed with jumpers, jeans,
with sacks of rice, tinned peaches, sticks
of gnarly biltong, little blister packs
of flucloxacillin and tetracycline.
We'll keep a diary as the world turns green.
Blackthorn is first to blow its stacks.
Whitethorn smells like sex in sleeping bags.
Hedgerows hum like old machines.
We'll listen for the song of frequent fliers
that build the distance with their calls
as midges braid in smoky coils
above the beck. We'll hardly hear
the motorway's soft and constant roar.
The tarp applauds like mad in summer hail.

3.

Horse mushrooms will appear in rings;
mist will roll in, like in a poem.
We'll look for sloes when winter comes
pinching the daylight out. I'll sing
while shaving on a cold morning,
you'll share the same mirror and comb
your hair, shivering, making plans to roam
and check the traps we set. The spring
comes round again – and what can stop
the trout from running in the beck,
the song of whitethroats and blackcaps,
the blossom on the crab apple,
the long evenings that turn purple
then fill with stars? I'll grow homesick

4.

listening to the motorway,
reading the small print on a tin
of peaches. I'll miss the pavements grey,
the push and shove of rush hours,
the fumy air in cities when
evening comes on, sudden downpours
and washed-out ruts of dirt, that haze
you get on certain August days,
these ripe and waspy wheelie bins,
this scruffy car park stung with flowers
powering down, bees in the rosebay
willowherb smudged with blue
like snooker players chalking their cues
building breaks, clearing the colours away.

# The Studio

Rinsing a brush, you think of the sea tonight
busy covering two-thirds of the Earth's surface.

Lighthouses are keeping an eye on it.
It holds a fraction of the human race.

Picturing it drained – grand canyons
all the way to Maine – gives you a gutted feeling.
An emptiness follows your curiosity.

Maybe it started with a children's Bible
where Moses parted the waters of the Red Sea.

You stared a hole into that illustration,
standing among the Israelites looking out
across the puddled path to the promised land.

The artist had even gone to the trouble
of fishes, flapping, wondering what just happened.

# Mascara

One used *chocolate*, one used *disinfectant*,
another swore by *Speke* . . . Anything would do.
*Anything* would do, and you'd get attached in the act
of repeating your word, until you'd worked it loose
from its sweet wrapper, a bottle beneath the sink,
or a timetable, stood at a blasted bus stop
repeating it, until your word was a thing
mouthed in the cold air, all its meaning gone.

The trick then was to break the spell and repair
the damage you'd done, or else find yourself stuck
with an empty cast, a fluttering font, sound hole
or hairline crack that led to the nameless world.
Those were the days we were so bored we'd break
anything. *Anything.* And even now
whenever I look my word straight in the vowels
there's nobody home. I get the blank stare.

# Memories of Midhope Street

*for Nick West*

I passed the interview for the room
then passed out in front of Sky News
after an evening in The Lamb with its snob screens
and legendary conventicles upstairs
with poets I'd yet to meet. When I took my brother
to see the flat on a rainy Good Friday
a woman straddled her punter on the stairwell
and we had to step over a tattooed buttock
carefully. The first months were an electric blanket
and the *Collected Poems* of Philip Larkin.
When my girlfriend moved in, we worried about a fire
so went to the chandler's in the Brunswick Centre
to buy a length of rope. The assistant smiled
recommending a silky, low friction twine, in black.

Somebody left a piano on the landing.
We were woken up by rough glissandos or 'Chopsticks'.
Going to work, we slipped on condoms or lemons.
We still got mail for a Japanese man who'd lived there
in the 1970s. When I went to confront
our upstairs neighbour for partying on a planked floor
I froze fish-eyed at our door
as one of his guests came down punching the air.

I bought my first computer and wrote every day.
Walking to the Tube through Argyle Square
and the view where Mrs Wilberforce had rooms to let
in *The Ladykillers* had hardly changed a bit.
Grimy extension cords, La Gitane sherry,
Ebony's budded skunk 'like veggie owl pellets'.
I was still in my twenties. I thought I'd ran my race.
An Apple Mac IIsi. The thrill of changing the typeface.

# Night Class

It's strange going back,
the corridors still shiny and mopped
to a smell and institutional squeak

not known to be conducive to poetry.
I can never find the room, and retrace
my steps. They're starting without me,

the teacher unclasping a briefcase
to produce a sandpiper, egg timer,
black silk vest, even a jaguar . . .

And I could so easily have missed it,
the janitor stacking chairs, the teacher
dead going on twenty years.

## My Last Drink

What'll it be? Vodka with a blade
of bison grass, to search the steppe for shade.

What's yours? Mezcal with a maguey grub
to chase big butterflies through the spiky scrub.

What are you having? Gin with borage flowers
to lead us up the garden path for hours.

No. Mine'll be a pint of lager pulled
from the nitrokeg of blackouts, salt and cold,

my usual. A musty cellar's tang,
the fizz of a licked battery on the tongue.

Down in one – I never did learn to pace
myself – I'll journey to the same old place

for one final first kiss, to hide in plain
sight looking a sight. The same, again.

# Cross Bedding, Between Edge Hill and Lime Street

*for Joyce Whitchurch*

I lose my place when the train passes Edge Hill,
where the unborn people who live in the metaphor
about getting off at Edge Hill crowd the platform
(metaphorically). As the tightened brakes take hold

like Larkin's passenger said, our long gone house
on Arrow Street is as real as the Edge Hill Iceland
that stands there now. The drivers do their best,
announcing that we'll reach our destination

in a few minutes. But I'm always gone by the time
we enter the mile of tunnel down to Lime Street,
cut in an age of coal riots and Factory Acts
and great symphonic works. Wet sandstone walls.

Am I outside of time, watching the flow
of vast unnamed rivers and giant dune systems?
The city's bedrock, up close, fills the windows
like Monument Valley in an aquarium.

*One Million Years B.C.* Or more a tearjerker,
like the cinema on the corner of Tunnel Road
(also long gone) is showing Triassic weepies.
That band of grey? A million years of rain.

And more the film of a book, a great stone volume
opened and read when this tunnel was first cut,
that I always lose my place in before I alight –
which sounds more like a stepping into light

than a descent. The odds against arriving
and being met under the clock. Who wrote
this poem of the film of the book of the earth
that shook when trains passed by our house at night?

∞

Look at you, playing hide and seek
    with whoever took this, on the steps
of a minaret – like a wedding cake
    meets a snail shell. Can you remember it?
Date palms, brickwork, the desert's glare,
    all captured by a shutter so fast
one second has filled up three albums.

    No? Me neither. I mean my own
beforetime. Just the sound of rain.
    If I struck a match on the wall of dark
that separates us, I could light a house,
    a hall. I could wind the clock, make mice
scratch in the skirting, trains go past.
    It's shaky, but that's me, on the stairs

carrying my unsteady flame.
    The shadows wheel. Can you see me yet?
I'm holding very still at the turn.
    The night listens in. The rain has stopped.
A trap clicks in the dark downstairs.
    The snuffed candle unwinds perfume
in long spirals. I'm saying my prayers.

# Bubblewrap

When I think of 'spots of time', I hear the tap
of rain on metal. I think of the den
I've built from cardboard sheets and bubblewrap
in the back of a removals van
being driven towards each different future.

A listing sofa, the rattling of mirrors,
a wardrobe kicking like a horse in its box.

Though these *are* only spots. Darkness surrounds them
and how we settled in on each first night
is as lost to me as a toothache or the chickenpox.
The time home took to germinate is gone.

*

After the recces, the viewings in daylight
with the unreliable narration of a landlord,
after the show houses seen in the magic hour,
this is the fumbling with a key in a lock,
this is *there must be a knack to it*,
these are the cold hands and the deed under frost,
this is the breath the house keeps to itself –
limewash, damp stone, old must, a trace of dog –
this is the short shrift of a hard echo,
both parties understandably on edge.
This is an existential housewarming
as we climbed the stairs unsure of what lay ahead.

*

Or maybe we slept soundly despite the journey,
despite the house's best nocturnal efforts.
A roof joist cracking. The pilot light bumping on.
The moon playing a silent film on the wall.
And maybe, at dawn, the first small fragile things
were unwrapped, the air turned intimate with radio
and the smell of fried bread . . .

                              Look how I wrap
myself in bubbles, a suit of soft lights.
Anything to stop it rubbing, to halt the chafe
as we walk out of the past. History will do that.
If I think of spots of time, to be exact,
I feel a crackle between my fingertips
and thumbs, between houses, lost in the act
of every happy and forgetful pop.

NOTES

'The Rout at Brunanburh' – the opening lines are loosely adapted from the Anglo-Saxon Chronicle's entry for A.D. 937 recording the Battle of Brunanburh, which might have been fought on the Wirral peninsula.

'Horde' – '(the horde, the spores of nowhere
Cultured under lamps and multiplied
In the laboratories
Between Mersey and Humber)'
— TED HUGHES 'On the Reservations'

'Corncrakes' – the poem quotes a line from 'An Bonnán Buí' by Cathal Buí Mac Giolla Ghunna, in Thomas MacDonagh's translation from the Irish.

'∞' – 'Cameras provide the option of focusing on a distance given as infinity. The equivalent shutter speed would, I suppose, be eternity.' — GEOFF DYER

'Cross Bedding, Between Edge Hill and Lime Street' – 'A review of *The Concise Scots Dictionary* that mentioned that "to get aff at Paisley" was a euphemism for coitus interruptus . . . brought a flood of correspondence reporting analogous local variants: for Merseysiders, "getting off at Edge Hill", the last station before

Liverpool Lime Street; "gettin' off at Haymarket", the station before Edinburgh Waverley; for sailors, "getting out at Fratton", the station before Portsmouth on the London line. "Travellers" might also be advised to ". . . always get off the bus at South Shore, don't go all the way to Blackpool".'  — Gigi Santow

'But who knew (other than paleontologists) that there was a time in Earth's history when it rained for a million years?'
— Rivka Galchen

ACKNOWLEDGEMENTS

Many thanks to the editors of the following journals and periodicals, where some of these poems first appeared: *Times Literary Supplement*, *Poetry London*, *London Review of Books*, *Explorations* (Poland). 'Tumbleweed' first appeared in *New Boots and Pantisocracies* as part of a chain sonnet (with thanks to Kathy Towers for providing a sturdy link). 'The Workaround' was first aired on The Verb (BBC Radio 4). 'The Studio' was included in the exhibition *Refractive Pool* at the Walker Art Gallery, Liverpool, as well as the catalogue that accompanied it, and my thanks to Brendan Lyons and Josie Jenkins for the invite. 'Bubblewrap' was originally written for *Walking Home*, part of the Wordsworth 250 celebrations, at the invitation of The Wordsworth Centre, Lancaster University. I'm grateful to Ross Raisin for allowing me to meddle with his sound advice, which provided some of the source material for 'Source'.

And thanks to Colette Bryce, Jacob Polley, and Carole Romaya.